"Half of what I say is meaningless;
but I say it so that the other half
may reach you."

Kahlil Gibran: The Poet-Philosopher Who Touched the World

Kahlil Gibran, a name synonymous with poetic genius and spiritual insight, was born on January 6, 1883, in the village of Bsharri, located in the stunning mountains of Lebanon. He was the third child of Khalil Gibran and Kamila Rahme, a loving couple who deeply valued education and literature. However, Gibran's childhood was not without its challenges.

At the age of eight, tragedy struck when Gibran's father, who worked as a tax collector, was unjustly imprisoned and subjected to investigation. The burden of providing for the family now fell on his mother, Kamila, who tirelessly worked as a seamstress to support her children. This early experience of hardship and injustice would later shape Gibran's worldview and fuel his creative expression.

Despite the difficulties, young Gibran displayed a remarkable curiosity and talent for art. Recognizing his potential, his mother encouraged his artistic pursuits, and he began drawing and sketching at an early age.
It was during this time that Gibran was first captivated by the natural beauty of his homeland—the rugged landscapes, the vibrant colors, and the profound connection between humanity and nature. These experiences would later become prominent themes in his writings.

Despite his father's release in 1894, Kahlil Gibran and his mother made the life-altering decision to immigrate to the United States in 1895 when he was twelve years old. They sought a better life and opportunities, eventually settling in the bustling city of Boston, Massachusetts, which would become their new home. The transition to a new culture and language was not easy for young Gibran, but he quickly adapted and found solace in his artistic endeavors.

In Boston, Gibran's artistic talent continued to flourish. He attended the Josiah Quincy School and also enrolled in an art school, where he honed his skills and expanded his creative horizons. It was during this time that a pivotal encounter took place at an exhibition of Gibran's drawings.

At the exhibition, Gibran had the fortune of crossing paths with Mary Elizabeth Haskell, a respected headmistress. Haskell recognized the immense potential in Gibran's work and became not only his mentor but also a source of emotional support and encouragement throughout his artistic journey.

Under Haskell's guidance, Gibran's poetic voice began to emerge. He experimented with various forms of writing, including prose, poetry, and essays, exploring themes of love, spirituality, and the human condition. His works began to garner attention and acclaim within literary circles.

In 1918, Gibran published his first major work, "The Madman," a collection of parables and poetic musings that offered profound insights into the nature of existence and the complexities of the human soul. The book received critical acclaim, establishing Gibran as a significant literary figure.

Alongside his literary success was a burgeoning career as a visual artist as well. He embraced the medium of painting and exhibited his works in renowned galleries across the United States. His paintings, often characterized by their mystical and spiritual themes, resonated with audiences, further solidifying his reputation as a multi-talented artist.

As Kahlil Gibran entered the latter part of his life, his profound insights into spirituality and the human experience continued to evolve, leaving an indelible mark on literature and philosophy.

In the early 1920s, Gibran's fame grew with the publication of his most celebrated work, "The Prophet," which would become his magnum opus. First published in 1923, this collection of poetic essays explored profound themes such as love, beauty, joy, sorrow, and self-realization. "The Prophet" captivated readers with its lyrical prose and timeless wisdom, becoming a global phenomenon and ultimately solidifying Gibran's place among the literary greats.

Gibran's spiritual teachings in "The Prophet" resonated deeply with people from diverse backgrounds and cultures. The book's universal themes spoke to the universal longing for inner peace and understanding.

Its popularity transcended borders, and translations of "The Prophet" soon made it accessible to readers worldwide.

Throughout his career, Gibran embraced the notion of unity and sought to bridge the gap between Eastern and Western philosophies. Influenced by his Lebanese heritage and exposure to Western thought, he synthesized his own unique brand of spirituality. Blending elements of Sufism, Christianity, and Eastern mysticism, Gibran created a holistic and inclusive worldview that resonated with individuals seeking solace and spiritual enlightenment.

Along the way, Gibran formed deep and meaningful friendships with prominent artists and personalities such as Carl Jung, Auguste Rodin, Rabindranath Tagore, and WB Yeats. These relationships provided him with invaluable intellectual stimulation and expanded his artistic horizons.

In his later years, Gibran faced health challenges, but his commitment to his artistic and spiritual endeavors remained unwavering. Despite the obstacles, he continued to write and paint, producing works that reflected his deepening insights into the human condition. His writings delved into themes such as mortality, the nature of time, and the eternal soul, showcasing his contemplation of profound existential questions.

Tragically, on April 10, 1931, at the age of 48, Kahlil Gibran passed away in New York City, leaving a void in the literary and artistic world. However, his impact and legacy endured long after his untimely death. His writings, paintings, and philosophical contributions continued to inspire generations to come.

The reach of Gibran's influence extended far beyond his lifetime, captivating readers across the globe and establishing him as one of the most widely read poets in history. Translated into over 100 languages, his works have sold millions of copies. Among them, "The Prophet" remains a perennial source of solace, inspiration, and spiritual guidance for countless individuals worldwide.

Gibran's profound influence can be observed in the works of subsequent generations of artists, writers, and philosophers. His unique fusion of Eastern and Western philosophies not only opened doors for intercultural dialogue but also expanded the understanding of spirituality in the modern world. Through his emphasis on love, compassion, and self-discovery, Gibran's words continue to resonate in an era marked by profound challenges and a profound search for meaning, touching the hearts and souls of countless individuals worldwide. His enduring legacy leaves an indelible mark on the literary and artistic landscape, shaping and inspiring generations to come.

Half of what I say is meaningless; but I say it so that the other half may reach you.

If you sing of beauty though alone in the heart of the desert you will have an audience.

They deem me mad because
I will not sell my days
for gold; and I deem them
mad because they think
my days have a price.

We measure time according to the movement of countless suns; and they measure time by little machines in their little pockets. Now tell me, how could we ever meet at the same place and the same time?

My loneliness was born
when men praised my
talkative faults and
blamed my silent
virtues.

The truly great man
is he who would master
no one, and who would
be mastered by none.

Beauty is not a need but
an ecstasy. It is not a
mouth thirsting nor an
empty hand stretched
forth, But rather
a heart enflamed and
a soul enchanted.

In truth we gaze but do not see, and hearken but do not hear; we eat and drink but do not taste. And there lies the difference between Jesus of Nazareth and ourselves. His senses were all continually made new, and the world to Him was always a new world.

Among the hills, when you sit
in the cool shade of the white
poplars, sharing the peace
and serenity of distant
fields and meadows – then let
your heart say in silence,
"God rests in reason."
And when the storm comes,
and the mighty wind shakes
the forest, and thunder and
lightning proclaim the
majesty of the sky, – then
let your heart say in awe,
"God moves in passion."

A thief is a
man in need.
A liar is a
man in fear.

Your daily life
is your temple
and your religion.
Whenever you enter
into it take with you
your all.

I have learned silence
from the talkative,
toleration from the
intolerant,
and kindness
from the unkind;
yet, strange, I am
ungrateful to those
teachers.

You pray in your distress
and in your need; would
that you might also pray
in the fullness of your
joy and in your days
of abundance.

When you reach the end
of what you should
know, you will be at
the beginning of what
you should sense.

Words are timeless.
You should utter them
or write them with a
knowledge of their
timelessness.

You are far, far greater
than you know – and all
is well.

Men who do not forgive
women their little faults
will never enjoy their
great virtues.

But let there be spaces
in your togetherness,
And let the winds of the heavens
dance between you.

Love one another,
but make not a bond of love:
Let it rather be a moving sea
between the shores of your souls.
Fill each other's cup
but drink not from one cup.
Give one another of your bread
but eat not from the same loaf.
Sing and dance together and be joyous,
but let each one of you be alone,
Even as the strings of a lute are alone
though they quiver with the same music.

That deepest thing, that recognition, that knowledge, that sense of kinship began the first time I saw you, and it is the same now – only a thousand times deeper and tenderer.
I shall love you to eternity.
I loved you long before we met in this flesh. I knew that when I first saw you. It was destiny. We are together like this and nothing can shake us apart.

Life without Liberty
is like a body without
spirit. Liberty without
thought is like a
disturbed spirit ... Life,
liberty, and thought —
three persons in one
substance, eternal,
never-ending, and
unceasing.

Said one oyster to a neighboring oyster, "I have a very great pain within me. It is heavy and round and I am in distress." And the other oyster replied with haughty complacence, "Praise be to the heavens and to the sea, I have no pain within me. I am well and whole both within and without." At that moment a crab was passing by and heard the two oysters, and he said to the one who was well and whole both within and without, "Yes, you are well and whole; but the pain that your neighbor bears is a pearl of exceeding beauty."

And could you keep your
heart in wonder at the
daily miracles of your
life, your pain would
not seem less wondrous
than your joy;
And you would accept the
seasons of your heart,
even as you have always
accepted the seasons
that pass over your
fields.

If you love somebody,
let them go, for if
they return, they
were always yours.
And if they don't,
they never were.

The universe is my
country and the
human family
is my tribe.

Keep me away from the wisdom which does not cry, the philosophy which does not laugh and the greatness which does not bow before children.

There must be something strangely sacred about salt. It is in our tears and in the sea.

If your heart is a volcano, how shall you expect flowers to bloom?

No man can draw the line
between necessities and
luxuries. Only the angels
can do that, and the angels
are wise and wistful.
Perhaps the angels are our
better thought in space.

We shall never
understand one
another until we
reduce the language
to seven words.

And God said,
Love your enemy,
& I obeyed Him
& loved myself.

Always have we been our own forerunners, and always shall we be. And all that we have gathered and shall gather shall be but seeds for fields yet unploughed. We are the fields and the ploughmen, the gatherers and the gathered.

Those who give you a
serpent when you ask for
a fish, may have nothing
but serpents to give.
It is then generosity
on their part.

Perhaps the sea's
definition of a shell
is the pearl.
Perhaps time's
definition of coal
is the diamond.

You give but little
when you give of
your possessions.
It is when you give
of yourself that you
truly give.

Work is love made visible. And if you cannot work with love but only with distaste, it is better that you should leave your work and sit at the gate of the temple and take alms of those who work with joy.

Limited love asks for possession of the beloved, but the unlimited asks only for itself. Love that comes between the naivete and awakening of youth satisfies itself with possessing, and grows with embraces. But Love which is born in the firmament's lap and has descended with the night's secrets is not contended with anything but Eternity and immortality; it does not stand reverently before anything except deity.

Your fear of death is but the trembling of the shepherd when he stands before the king whose hand is to be laid upon him in honour.

And if you would know
God, be not therefore a
solver of riddles. Rather
look about you and you
shall see Him playing
with your children. And
look into space; you shall
see Him walking in the
cloud, outstretching His
arms in the lightning and
descending in rain. You
shall see Him smiling in
flowers, then rising and
waving His hands in trees.

From a sensitive woman's heart springs the happiness of mankind, and from the kindness of her noble spirit comes mankind's affection.

It is wrong to think that love comes from long companionship and persevering courtship. Love is the offspring of spiritual affinity and unless that affinity is created in a moment, it will not be created for years or even generations.

A little knowledge
that acts is worth
infinitely more than
much knowledge
that is idle.

Desire is
half of life,
indifference
is half of death.

We are expression of earth, and of life – not separate individuals only. We cannot get enough away from the earth to see the earth and ourselves as separates. We move with its great movements and our growth is part of its great growth.

The deeper that sorrow
carves into your being, the
more joy you can contain.
Is not the cup that holds
your wine the very cup
that was burned in the
potter's oven?
And is not the lute that
soothes your spirit,
the very wood that was
hollowed with knives?

When a man's hand
touches the hand of a
woman, they both touch
the heart of eternity.

Doubt is a pain too
lonely to know that
faith is his twin
brother.

For thought is a bird
of space, that in a cage
of words may indeed
unfold its wings
but cannot fly.

The first thought
of God was an angel.
The first word of God
was a man.

The nearest to my
heart are a king
without a kingdom and
a poor man who does
not know how to beg.

You cannot judge
any man beyond your
knowledge of him,
and how small
is your knowledge.

You may forget with
whom you laughed, but
you will never forget
with whom you wept.

To belittle,
you have to be little.

Every thing in nature bespeaks
the mother. The sun is the
mother of earth and gives it its
nourishment of hear; it never
leaves the universe at night
until it has put the earth to
sleep to the song of the sea and
the hymn of birds and brooks.
And this earth is the mother of
trees and flowers. It produces
them, nurses them, and weans
them. The trees and flowers
become kind mothers of their
great fruits and seeds. And the
mother, the prototype of all
existence, is the eternal spirit,
full of beauty and love.

All can hear, but
only the sensitive
can understand.

How often have you
sailed in my dreams.
And now you come in
my awakening, which
is my deeper dream.

Every man is two men;
one is awake in the
darkness, the other
asleep in the light.

If you reveal your
secrets to the wind,
you should not blame
the wind for revealing
them to the trees.

I deserted the world and sought solitude because I became tired of rendering courtesy to those multitudes who believe that humility is a sort of weakness, and mercy a kind of cowardice, and snobbery a form of strength.

That which is
boundless in you
abides in the mansion
of the sky, whose door
is the morning mist,
and whose windows
are the songs and the
silences of night.

One may not reach
the dawn save by
the path of the
night.

And ever has it
been known that
love knows not its
own depth until the
hour of separation.

The appearance
of things change
according to the
emotions, and thus we
see magic and beauty
in them, while the
magic and beauty are
really in ourselves.

Yesterday we obeyed
kings and bent our
necks before emperors.
But today we
kneel only to truth,
follow only beauty,
and obey only love.

Are you a politician asking what your country can do for you or a zealous one asking what you can do for your country? If you are the first, then you are a parasite; if the second, then you are an oasis in the desert.

Vague and nebulous is the beginning of all things, but not their end, And I fain would have you remember me as a beginning. Life, and all that lives, is conceived in the mist and not in the crystal. And who knows but a crystal is mist in decay?

I have found both freedom and safety in my madness; the freedom of loneliness and the safety from being understood, for those who understand us enslave something in us.

The Sphinx spoke
only once, and the
Sphinx said, "A grain
of sand is a desert,
and a desert is a
grain of sand; and
now let us all be
silent again."

Jesus was not sent here to teach the people to build magnificent churches and temples amidst the cold wretched huts and dismal hovels. He came to make the human heart a temple, and the soul an altar, and the mind a priest.

My yearning is my cup,
my burning thirst is my
drink, and my solitude
is my intoxication;
I do not and shall
not quench my thirst.
But in this burning that
is never extinguished
is a joy that never
wanes.

You shall be free indeed
when your days are not
without a care, nor your
nights without a want
and a grief, but rather
when these things girdle
your life and yet you
rise above them naked
and unbound.

Truth is like the stars; it does not appear except from behind obscurity of the night. Truth is like all beautiful things in the world; it does not disclose its desirability except to those who first feel the influence of falsehood. Truth is a deep kindness that teaches us to be content in our everyday life and share with the people the same happiness.

The timeless in you
is aware of life's
timelessness. And
knows that yesterday
is but today's memory
and tomorrow is
today's dream.

Love is a magic ray
emitted from the
burning core of the soul
and illuminating the
surrounding earth. It
enables us to perceive
life as a beautiful
dream between one
awakening and another.

When love beckons to you
follow him, Though his
ways are hard and steep.
And when his wings enfold
you yield to him, Though
the sword hidden among
his pinions may wound
you. And when he speaks to
you believe in him, Though
his voice may shatter your
dreams as the north wind
lays waste the garden. For
even as love crowns you
so shall he crucify you.

Persecution cannot harm him who stands by Truth. Did not Socrates fall proudly a victim in body? Was not Paul stoned for the sake of the Truth? It is our inner selves that hurt us when we disobey it, and it kills us when we betray it.

Give your hearts, but not
into each other's keeping.
For only the hand of Life
can contain your hearts.
And stand together yet not
too near together:
For the pillars of the
temple stand apart,
And the oak tree and the
cypress grow not in each
other's shadow.

It was but yesterday
I thought myself a
fragment quivering
without rhythm in the
sphere of life. Now I
know that I am the
sphere, and all life in
rhythmic fragments
moves within me.

The reality of the other person is not in what he reveals to you, but in what he cannot reveal to you. Therefore, if you would understand him, listen not to what he says but rather to what he does not say.

Pity the nation whose statesman is a fox, whose philosopher is a juggler, and whose art is the art of patching and mimicking. Pity the nation that welcomes its new ruler with trumpetings, and farewells him with hootings, only to welcome another ruler with trumpetings again. Pity the nation whose sages are dumb with years and whose strong men are yet in the cradle. Pity the nation divided into fragments, each fragment deeming itself a nation.

Your thought advocates Judaism, Brahmanism, Buddhism, Christianity, and Islam. In my thought there is only one universal religion, whose varied paths are but the fingers of the loving hand of the Supreme Being. In your thought there are the rich, the poor, and the beggared. My thought holds that there are no riches but life; that we are all beggars, and no benefactor exists save life herself.

The heart's affections
are divided like the
branches of the cedar
tree; if the tree loses
one strong branch;
it will suffer but it
does not die; it will
pour all its vitality
into the next branch so
that it will grow and
fill the empty place.

My Soul gave me good counsel, teaching me never to delight in praise or to be distressed by reproach. Before my Soul taught me, I doubted the value of my accomplishments until the passing days sent someone who would extol or disparage them. But now I know that trees blossom in the spring and give their fruits in the summer without any desire for accolades. And they scatter their leaves abroad in the fall and denude themselves in the winter without fear of reproof.

Love gives naught but itself and takes naught but from itself. Love possesses not nor would it be possessed; For love is sufficient unto love... And think not you can direct the course of love, for love, if it finds you worthy, directs your course.

It is well to give
when asked, but
it is better to give
unasked, through
understanding; and to
the open-handed the
search for one who
shall receive is joy
greater than giving.

Beauty is that which attracts your soul, and that which loves to give and not receive. When you meet Beauty, you feel that the hands deep within your inner self are stretched forth to bring her into the domain of your heart. It is a magnificence combined of sorrow and joy; it is the Unseen which you see, and the Vague which you understand, and the Mute which you hear—it is the Holy of Holies that begins in yourself and ends vastly beyond your earthly imagination.

I would not exchange
the sorrows of my heart
For the joys of the multitude.
And I would not have the tears
that sadness makes
To flow from my every part
turn into laughter.

I would that my life remain
a tear and a smile.

A tear to purify my heart
and give me understanding
Of life's secrets and hidden things.
A smile to draw me nigh
to the sons of my kind and
To be a symbol of my glorification
of the gods.

A tear to unite me
with those of broken heart;
A smile to be a sign of my joy in
existence.

You cannot lay remorse upon the innocent nor lift it from the heart of the guilty. Unbidden shall it call in the night, that men may wake and gaze upon themselves.

Trees are poems the earth writes upon the sky, We fell them down and turn them into paper, That we may record our emptiness.

Your children are not your children. They are the sons and daughters of Life's longing for itself. They come through you but not from you, and though they are with you, yet they belong not to you. You may give them your love, but not your thoughts. For they have their own thoughts. You may house their bodies but not their souls, for their souls dwell in the house of tomorrow, which you cannot visit, not even in your dreams. You may strive to be like them, but seek not to make them like you. For life goes not backward, nor tarries with yesterday.

When you are joyous,
look deep into your
heart and you shall find
it is only that which
has given you sorrow
that is giving you joy.
When you are sorrowful
look again in your
heart, and you shall see
that in truth you are
weeping for that which
has been your delight.

Your pain is the breaking
of the shell that encloses
your understanding. Even
as the stone of the fruit
must break, that its heart
may stand in the sun, so
must you know pain.

To wake at dawn with a
winged heart and give
thanks for another day
of loving;
To rest at the noon hour and
meditate love's ecstasy;
To return home in the
eventide with gratitude;
And then to sleep with a
prayer for the beloved in
your heart and a song of
praise upon your lips.

You have been told that, even like a chain, you are as weak as your weakest link. This is but half the truth. You are also as strong as your strongest link. To measure you by your smallest deed is to reckon the power of ocean by the frailty of its foam. To judge you by your failures is to cast blame upon the seasons for their inconstancy.

For what is prayer but
the expansion of yourself
into the living ether?
And if it is for your
comfort to pour your
darkness into space, it is
also for your delight to
pour forth the dawning of
your heart.

We wanderers, ever seeking the lonelier way, begin no day where we have ended another, and no sunrise finds us where left by sunset. Even while the earth sleeps we travel. We are the seeds of that tenacious plant, and it is in our ripeness and our fullness of heart that we are given to the wind to be scattered.

Vain are the beliefs and teachings that make man miserable, and false is the goodness that leads him into sorrow and despair, for it is man's purpose to be happy on this earth and lead the way to felicity and preach its gospel wherever he goes. He who does not see the kingdom of heaven in this life will never see it in the coming life. We came not into this life by exile, but we came as innocent creatures of God, to learn how to worship the holy and eternal spirit and seek the hidden secrets within ourselves from the beauty of life. This is the truth which I have learned from the teachings of the Nazarene.

In the sweetness of friendship let there be laughter, and sharing of pleasures. For in the dew of little things the heart finds its morning and is refreshed.

Generosity is giving more than you can, and pride is taking less than you need.

Only an idiot and a genius break man-made laws; and they are the nearest to the heart of God.

Money is like a stringed instrument; he who does not know how to use it properly will hear only discordant music. Money is like love; it kills slowly and painfully the one who withholds it, and enlivens the other who turns it on his fellow man.

I believe that you can say to Abraham Lincoln, the blessed, "Jesus of Nazareth touched your lips when you spoke, and guided your hand when you wrote; and I shall uphold all that you have said and all that you have written."
I believe that you can say to Emerson and Whitman and James, "In my veins runs the blood of the poets and wise men of old, and it is my desire to come to you and receive, but I shall not come with empty hands."

All that you see was
and is for your sake. The
numerous books, uncanny
markings, and beautiful
thoughts are the ghosts of
souls who preceded you.
The speech they weave is a
link between you and
your human siblings.
The consequences that
cause sorrow and rapture
are the seeds that the past
has sown in the field of
the soul, and by which the
future shall profit.

In the depth
of my soul there is
A wordless song –
a song that lives
In the seed of my heart.
It refuses to melt with
ink on Parchment; it
engulfs my affection
In a transparent
cloak and flows,
But not upon my lips.

When you part from your friend, you grieve not; For that which you love most in him may be clearer in his absence, as the mountain to the climber is clearer from the plain.

Glimpses into Gibran's World: Intriguing Facts about the Iconic Poet

Kahlil Gibran's early childhood was marked by adversity. His father was arrested for embezzlement, which caused a significant upheaval in the family. Along with his mother and siblings, Gibran emigrated to Boston, seeking a better life and leaving behind their homeland of Lebanon. This experience of immigration and the challenges it brought would shape Gibran's perspective and inspire much of his later work.

At the age of 15, Gibran was sent back to Lebanon to study Arabic literature, providing him with an opportunity to reconnect with his cultural roots and deepen his understanding of his native language and literature. However, tragedy struck when his sister and half-brother passed away, followed by the loss of his mother. Devastated by these losses, Gibran eventually returned to the United States. During this difficult time, his remaining sister played a pivotal role in supporting him both financially and emotionally, helping him navigate through his grief and find solace.

Mary Haskell, a significant figure in Gibran's life, served as both a patron and a close companion. She recognized his artistic talent and provided him with financial support and encouragement. Haskell's influence was instrumental in shaping Gibran's artistic journey.

Under her patronage, he had the opportunity to study art in Paris from 1908 to 1910, allowing him to expand his artistic skills and explore new creative horizons.

Gibran was fluent in several languages, including Arabic, English, and French. This linguistic versatility allowed him to express his thoughts and ideas with nuance and reach a diverse range of readers. His proficiency in multiple languages facilitated his ability to connect with different cultures and enriched the depth and breadth of his literary and artistic contributions.

Gibran drew inspiration from a variety of sources, and two notable influences on his work were Francis Marrash and Walt Whitman. Marrash, a Syrian poet and philosopher, played a significant role in introducing French romanticism to the Arab world. His writings, which included poetic prose and prose poetry, were among the first examples of these forms in modern Arabic literature. Marrash's fusion of Arabic language and French literary techniques expanded the possibilities of expression for Gibran and other Arab writers, influencing their approach to form, style, and symbolism.

Walt Whitman, the renowned American poet, also left an indelible impact on Gibran's writing. Whitman's celebration of individualism, spiritual exploration, and his unique poetic style influenced Gibran's own artistic sensibilities. Gibran found inspiration in Whitman's ability to express profound ideas through poetic language and embraced a similar approach in his own works, infusing them with a sense of personal reflection and universal wisdom.

Kahlil Gibran was a multi-talented artist who expressed himself through various mediums. Alongside his literary achievements, he also showcased his artistic skills through visual art exhibitions. When he was 15, a publisher recognized his talent and utilized some of Gibran's artwork for book covers in 1898. This early recognition highlighted his artistic versatility and marked the beginning of his journey as a visual artist. Throughout his career, Gibran's works were shown in galleries and exhibitions, solidifying his reputation as a prolific visual artist. His ability to convey his thoughts and emotions through different artistic forms, be it writing or visual art, allowed him to create a rich tapestry of expression that continues to captivate audiences.

Gibran formed a close friendship with the renowned French sculptor Auguste Rodin. Rodin held Gibran in high regard, referring to him as 'the Blake of the 20th century.' This association with Rodin not only symbolized the recognition and respect Gibran received from fellow artists but also showcased the profound impact of his art and writings on the artistic community of his time. The friendship with Rodin further enriched Gibran's artistic journey and contributed to his legacy as a visionary artist.

Kahlil Gibran's profound writings resonated with many artists and musicians, including the legendary musician John Lennon. Lennon drew inspiration from Gibran's work and incorporated a line from Gibran's book "Sand and Foam" into his song "Julia."

The line "Half of what I say is meaningless" added a touch of Gibran's insightful philosophy to Lennon's song, demonstrating the impact and enduring relevance of Gibran's words on other artistic minds. In addition to Lennon, Gibran's influence extends to other renowned figures such as Elvis Presley, Johnny Cash, David Bowie, and many more.

"The Prophet" stands as one of Kahlil Gibran's most iconic works and has achieved remarkable success in terms of sales and translation. It remains one of the best-selling books of all time, with translations available in over 100 languages. The profound wisdom and poetic beauty contained within "The Prophet" have captivated readers worldwide, making it a beloved and influential literary masterpiece.

Kahlil Gibran's literary contributions have solidified his place as one of the most widely read poets in history. His profound insights into love, spirituality, and the human condition have resonated with countless readers across generations. Gibran's popularity and enduring appeal have positioned him as the third most widely read poet, following the timeless works of Shakespeare and Lao-Tzu, further cementing his literary legacy.

Despite his popularity among readers, Kahlil Gibran faced neglect from Western scholars and critics for a significant period. His works were not given the attention and recognition they deserved in academic circles.

However, this trend gradually changed as more scholars and critics began to appreciate the depth and significance of Gibran's writings, leading to a reassessment of his contributions to literature and philosophy.

Kahlil Gibran shares a familial connection with the renowned American sculptor Kahlil G. Gibran. They were cousins, sharing not only a name but also a creative lineage. The artistic talents of both individuals underscore the artistic legacy within their family, with each making their own unique contributions to their respective fields.

Kahlil Gibran's life was tragically cut short at the age of 48. The cause of his death was reported as cirrhosis of the liver, compounded by incipient tuberculosis in one of his lungs. It is believed that his excessive drinking contributed to his deteriorating health. Despite his untimely demise, Gibran had already achieved literary fame on "both sides of the Atlantic Ocean." His works had garnered widespread recognition and acclaim, leaving an indelible mark on the literary landscape and ensuring his enduring legacy as a profound writer and philosopher.

This section offers readers a glimpse into Kahlil Gibran's most significant works, followed by an exploration of his important themes and ideas.

The Prophet (1923)

"The Prophet" is a timeless literary work written by Kahlil Gibran, originally published in 1923. This collection of poetic essays has since become one of Gibran's most celebrated and influential works, touching the hearts and minds of readers around the world.

"The Prophet" consists of twenty-six prose poems, each exploring different aspects of human existence and the human condition. The book takes the form of a conversation between Almustafa, a prophet and wise figure, and a group of people who seek his insights and guidance. Through these conversations, Gibran delves into profound themes such as love, beauty, joy, sorrow, freedom, and self-realization.

One of the defining qualities of "The Prophet" is its lyrical and evocative prose. Gibran's writing style is poetic and rich in symbolism, drawing readers into a contemplative and reflective journey. The words flow effortlessly, capturing the essence of profound emotions and existential questions. Each prose poem acts as a standalone piece, yet they come together to form a cohesive exploration of life's complexities and universal truths.

Love is a central theme throughout "The Prophet." Gibran explores love in its various forms, including romantic love, love for family and friends, and love for humanity as a whole.

He delves into the transformative power of love, its ability to bring joy and fulfillment, as well as its capacity to cause pain and longing. Gibran's reflections on love resonate deeply with readers, offering insights into the profound connections that bind us together as human beings.

Spirituality is another significant aspect of "The Prophet." Gibran draws from diverse religious and philosophical traditions, infusing his writings with elements of Sufism, Christianity, and Eastern mysticism. Through his poetic language, he invites readers to explore their own spiritual paths and seek a deeper understanding of their place in the universe. The book's spiritual teachings transcend religious boundaries, emphasizing the universal nature of the human quest for meaning and enlightenment.

"The Prophet" became a global phenomenon, transcending cultural and linguistic barriers. Translations of the book made it accessible to readers worldwide, and its popularity continues to endure to this day. Readers from different backgrounds and walks of life have found solace, inspiration, and guidance within its pages. The timeless wisdom and universal themes explored in "The Prophet" make it a source of contemplation and reflection for generations.

Beyond its literary impact, "The Prophet" has influenced various art forms and has been adapted into stage plays, musical compositions, and visual artworks. The profound and evocative nature of Gibran's words has inspired countless artists, writers, and thinkers, further cementing the book's enduring legacy.

The Broken Wings (1912)

"Broken Wings", a novella published in 1912, tells a tragic love story that takes place in Beirut at the turn of the 20th century. The central character, a young man reminiscent of Kahlil Gibran himself, becomes enamored with Selma Karamy, a woman who is engaged to the nephew of a prominent religious figure. Despite the social constraints and the impending arranged marriage, the young man and Selma begin a clandestine relationship, cherishing their secret meetings.

However, their happiness is short-lived as their relationship is discovered, leading to dire consequences. Selma is forbidden from leaving her house, effectively putting an end to their hopes and dreams. The story revolves around the heartbreak and longing experienced by the protagonist and Selma as they grapple with the societal restrictions and the shattered possibilities of their love.

Throughout the novella, "Broken Wings" explores themes of forbidden love, societal expectations, and the emotional turmoil caused by the collision of personal desires and social conventions. Gibran's evocative prose captures the anguish and yearning of the two lovers, painting a poignant picture of the sacrifices made in the name of tradition and duty.

In this tragic tale, Gibran masterfully conveys the complexities of human emotions, delving into the depths of longing, loss, and the bittersweet nature of forbidden love. "Broken Wings" serves as a powerful exploration of the human spirit's resilience in the face of adversity and the enduring impact of unfulfilled love.

A Tear and a Smile (1914)

"A Tear and a Smile" is a remarkable collection of poems and short essays by Kahlil Gibran, originally published in 1914. Within this captivating compilation, Gibran skillfully weaves together the tapestry of human emotions and experiences, exploring the profound duality of human existence—the interplay between tears and smiles.

Throughout "A Tear and a Smile," Gibran delves into the power of tears to unite individuals who have experienced broken hearts and endured the trials of life. With his poignant verses, he offers solace and understanding to those who have known sorrow, reminding them that their tears are not solitary, but rather a shared human experience. Gibran's words resonate with empathy, providing comfort to those who carry the weight of their own grief.

In contrast, Gibran exalts the profound significance of love and joy in existence. He keenly acknowledges their transformative power, capable of uplifting spirits, bridging divides, and fostering deep connections. Through his masterful use of lyrical prose and evocative imagery, Gibran invites readers to wholeheartedly embrace the inherent beauty of life, finding solace and boundless inspiration in moments of happiness and serene tranquility.

Within the pages of "A Tear and a Smile," Gibran masterfully explores the intricacies of the human condition, illuminating the intertwined nature of sorrow and joy. His words serve as a poignant reminder that both tears and smiles are essential threads in the tapestry of our lives.

They represent the depth and complexity of our emotions, and they unite us in our shared humanity.

This remarkable collection showcases Gibran's poetic language, capturing the essence of the human experience. It encourages readers to reflect on their own tears and smiles, offering profound insights into the universal longing for connection, understanding, and fulfillment. "A Tear and a Smile" stands as a testament to the enduring power of poetry to touch our hearts, inspire contemplation, and remind us of the inherent beauty that resides within the rich tapestry of our lives.

The Madman (1918)

"The Madman," a captivating collection of parables and poems written by Kahlil Gibran and published in 1918, delves into profound themes that encompass the essence of human experience. Through its pages, readers are invited to embark on a journey that explores the intricacies of love, loss, spirituality, and the nature of truth. Gibran's insightful and evocative prose illuminates the depths of human emotions, inviting contemplation and reflection.

Within "The Madman," Gibran skillfully captures the complexities of love, navigating its joys, sorrows, and transformative power. Through his poetic language, he delves into the depths of the heart, painting vivid portraits of longing, passion, and the intricacies of human connection.

Loss, a universal human experience, finds its place in the collection as well.

Gibran's poignant words offer solace and understanding to those who have tasted the bitterness of loss, guiding them on a path of healing and acceptance. He explores the profound impact of loss on the human spirit, reminding readers of the resilience and strength that can emerge from such trials.

Spirituality weaves its way through the tapestry of "The Madman." Gibran's writings evoke a sense of wonder and contemplation, encouraging readers to delve into the mysteries of existence and forge their own spiritual paths. Through his prose, he invites a deeper connection with the divine and a recognition of the sacred in everyday life.

At the heart of "The Madman" lies the quest for truth. Gibran challenges established notions and invites readers to question their own beliefs and perceptions. His profound musings inspire introspection, urging individuals to seek their own inner truth and to embrace the fluidity and complexity of human understanding.

Gibran's insightful and evocative prose captivates readers, leading them on a thought-provoking exploration of the depths of human emotions and the complexities of existence. "The Madman" stands as a testament to his mastery of language and his ability to touch the hearts and minds of readers with his profound insights. It is a work that continues to resonate, inviting us to reflect on our own lives, beliefs, and the profound mysteries that shape our shared human journey.

Sand and Foam (1926)

"I Am Forever walking upon these shores,
Betwixt the sand and the foam,
The high tide will erase my footprints,
And the wind will blow away the foam.
But the sea and the shore will remain
Forever."

These captivating lines introduce "Sand and Foam," a profound collection of aphorisms and philosophical reflections by Kahlil Gibran. Published in 1926, the book invites readers on a contemplative journey, exploring the eternal dance between transient existence and the enduring elements of life.

Gibran's poetic wisdom shines through the pages of "Sand and Foam," as he delves into the depths of human experience and offers insights into the nature of existence. Each aphorism is a compact expression of profound thought, inviting readers to reflect on the complexities of life, love, and the human condition.

The imagery of walking upon the shores, with the sand representing the transient moments and the foam symbolizing the fleeting experiences, sets the tone for introspection. Gibran acknowledges the impermanence of individual footprints and the ephemeral nature of the foam blown by the wind. However, he reminds us that amidst the transitory aspects of life, the sea and the shore remain steadfast, representing the timeless and enduring forces that shape our existence.

Throughout "Sand and Foam," Gibran contemplates various facets of life, love, nature, sorrow, and spirituality. His aphorisms touch upon themes of self-discovery, relationships, freedom, beauty, and the pursuit of truth. With lyrical prose and evocative imagery, he challenges conventional wisdom and invites readers to seek deeper meaning and purpose in their lives.

The aphorisms in "Sand and Foam" are like gems of insight, offering glimpses into the mysteries of the human experience. They encourage readers to question societal norms, expand their perspectives, and embrace the inherent beauty of the world. Gibran's words resonate with timeless truths, inviting readers to explore their own thoughts, emotions, and connections to the world around them.

Kahlil Gibran's Major themes and Ideas

In the works of Kahlil Gibran, we find a tapestry of profound themes and ideas that resonate deeply with readers. His writings delve into the depths of human existence, exploring love, spirituality, unity, and the complexities of life. Within the pages of his books, Gibran's words paint vivid images and evoke emotions that touch the core of our being. In this section, we will delve further into ten prominent themes that emerge from his works, offering a glimpse into the wisdom and insights he imparts to his readers.

PERSISTENT FAITH IN LOVE: Kahlil Gibran's writings embody a persistent faith in the power of love. He explores love in its various forms, including romantic love, love for humanity, and spiritual love.

Gibran's works emphasize the transformative nature of love, its ability to heal and bring joy, and its capacity to guide individuals through life's challenges. Through his words, Gibran instills a deep belief in the enduring and transformative power of love, encouraging readers to embrace it as a guiding force in their lives.

LOVE OF NATURE: Nature holds a special place in Gibran's works. He expresses a profound love and appreciation for the natural world, celebrating its beauty, harmony, and wisdom. Gibran sees nature as a source of inspiration and spiritual insight. Through his writings, he invites readers to connect with nature, to witness its splendor, and to recognize the interconnectedness between humans and the natural world. Gibran's love of nature serves as a reminder of the inherent beauty that surrounds us and encourages a deeper connection with the environment.

SPIRITUALITY AND MYSTICISM: Gibran's writings delve into spirituality and mysticism, exploring the realms beyond the material world. He invites readers to embark on a journey of self-discovery and spiritual enlightenment, encouraging them to seek a deeper understanding of the mysteries of existence. Gibran's works often incorporate mystical elements and symbolism, evoking a sense of wonder and awe. Through his words, he inspires individuals to explore their spiritual essence, find inner peace, and connect with the divine.

UNITY AND INTERCONNECTEDNESS: Gibran's philosophy emphasizes the unity and interconnectedness of all beings. He sees humanity as part of a larger whole, intimately connected through shared experiences and emotions. Gibran's writings promote empathy, compassion, and a sense of unity among individuals.

He highlights the importance of harmonious coexistence and the ripple effects of our actions in the interconnected web of life. Gibran's words inspire readers to recognize the inherent connections that bind us together and to cultivate a sense of unity in their interactions with others.

PEACE AND EMPATHY: Gibran's works advocate for peace and empathy in human relationships and society as a whole. He emphasizes the importance of understanding, compassion, and kindness in fostering harmonious connections. Gibran encourages readers to approach conflicts with empathy and seek peaceful resolutions. His writings inspire individuals to cultivate inner peace and extend it to others, promoting a more compassionate and harmonious world.

WISDOM OF THE HEART: Gibran places great importance on the wisdom that resides within the heart. He values intuition, emotional intelligence, and the ability to connect with one's innermost feelings and desires. Gibran's writings encourage readers to listen to the voice of the heart, as it holds valuable insights and guidance for navigating life's challenges. He invites individuals to tap into their inner wisdom, trusting the profound knowledge that resides within them.

BALANCE AND HARMONY: Gibran's philosophy promotes the pursuit of balance and harmony in all aspects of life. He encourages individuals to find equilibrium between various aspects, such as work and leisure, solitude and social interaction, and the material and spiritual realms. Gibran emphasizes the interconnectedness of these aspects and the importance of maintaining a sense of equilibrium to foster overall well-being.

Through his words, he inspires readers to seek balance and harmony in their lives, allowing them to lead fulfilled and meaningful existences.

TIME AND TRANSCIENCE: Gibran contemplates the nature of time and the fleeting nature of human existence. He reflects on the impermanence of worldly things, emphasizing the need to appreciate the present moment and detach oneself from attachments to material possessions. Gibran's writings encourage readers to seek a deeper understanding of the eternal aspects of life beyond the constraints of time. He invites individuals to embrace the transience of life and find meaning in the fleeting moments.

FREEDOM AND INDIVIDUALITY: Gibran celebrates personal freedom and the uniqueness of individuals. He challenges societal norms and encourages individuals to break free from the constraints imposed by society. Gibran's writings emphasize the beauty of embracing one's true self and living authentically. He values freedom of thought, expression, and self-determination, inspiring readers to forge their own paths and embrace their individuality.

JOY AND SORROW: Gibran explores the duality of joy and sorrow in the human experience. He acknowledges the inevitability of pain, loss, and hardship, but also emphasizes the potential for growth and transformation that can arise from these experiences. Gibran's writings encourage readers to embrace both the sorrows and joys of life, recognizing that they are integral parts of the human journey. He invites individuals to find meaning and purpose in both the moments of happiness and the lessons learned through adversity.

Made in the USA
Las Vegas, NV
19 January 2024

84584751R00069